DOG LOVERS COLORING BOOK

Featuring:
LABRADOR RETRIEVERS

Copyright 2017

I am America's favorite pooch

My name is a little misleading

I come from Newfoundland, not Labrador

I'm extremely social and I love everyone

I'm the most commonly used breed as guide dogs

I have a very
high pain threshold
so I'm excellent
at rescue work

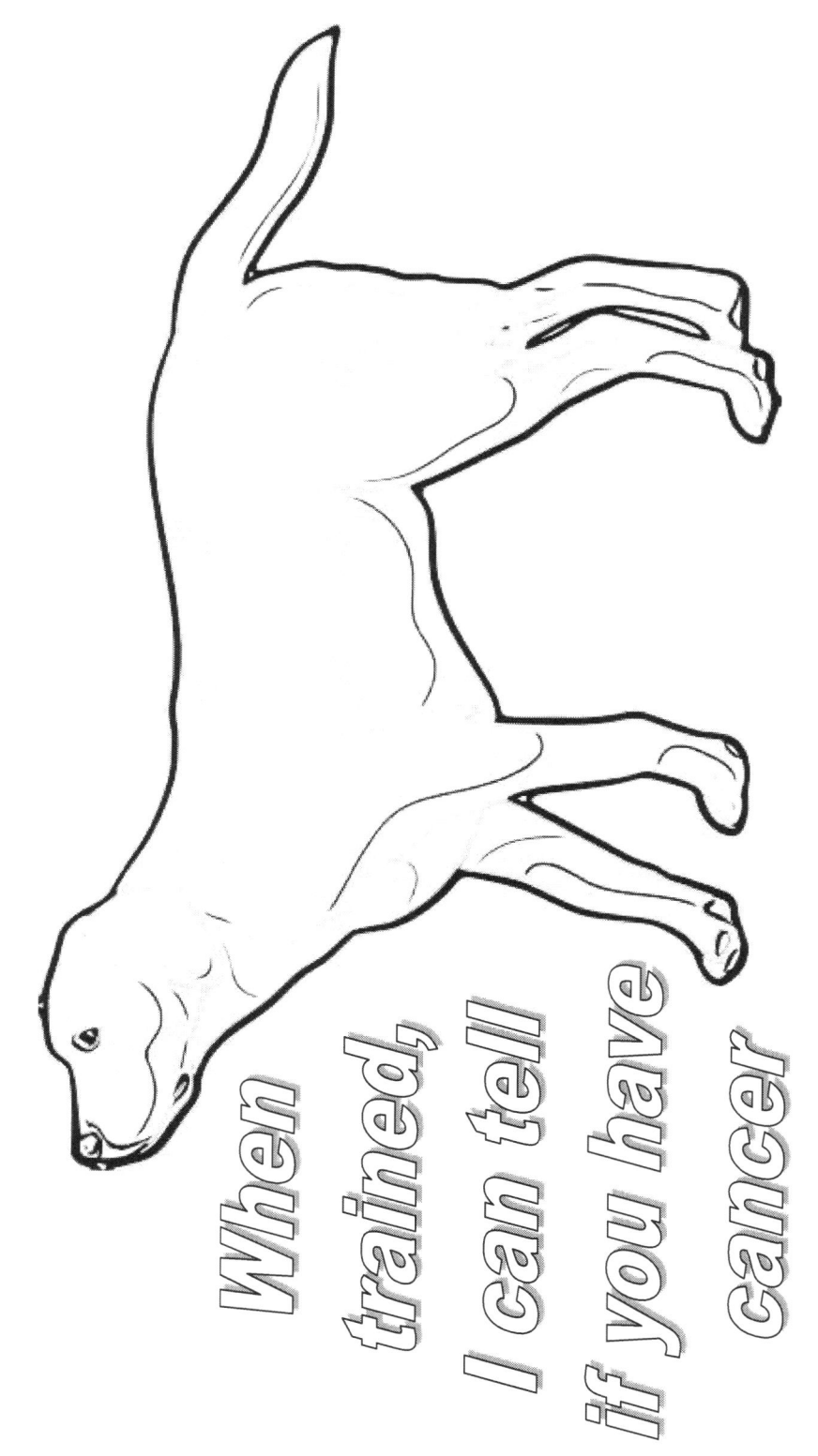

When trained, I can tell if you have cancer

I'm outgoing, gentle agile, intelligent, & even tempered

I need lots of exercise, not just short walks

I mature slowly, remaining a spirited teenager for many years

I am eager to please

I have high energy when I'm young, I romp & I jump with vigor

I am peaceful with other animals

I LUV
MY LAB!

Printed in Great Britain
by Amazon

34255977R00018